PAUL REVERE'S MIDNIGHT RIDE

BY STEPHEN KRENSKY

ILLUSTRATIONS BY GREG HARLIN

★

HarperCollinsPublishers

*For all the Lexington Minutemen,
past and present*

—S.K.

*To my father, Douglas Harlin,
who continues to teach me about
perseverance through trials*

—G.H.

Paul Revere's Midnight Ride
Text copyright © 2002 by Stephen Krensky
Illustrations copyright © 2002 by Greg Harlin
Printed in Hong Kong. All rights reserved.
www.harperchildrens.com
Library of Congress Cataloging-in-Publication Data
Krensky, Stephen.
Paul Revere's Midnight Ride / by Stephen Krensky ;
illustrations by Greg Harlin.
p.   cm.
ISBN 0-688-16409-9—ISBN 0-688-16410-2 (lib. bdg.)
1. Revere, Paul, 1735–1818—Juvenile literature.   2. Massachusetts—History—
Revolution, 1775–1783—Juvenile literature.   3. Lexington, Battle of, 1775—
Juvenile literature.   4. Concord, Battle of, 1775—Juvenile literature.   [1. Revere,
Paul, 1735–1818.   2. Massachusetts—History—Revolution, 1775–1783.
3. United States—History—Revolution, 1775–1783.]
I. Harlin, Greg, ill.   II. Title.
F69.R43 K74   2002   973.3'311'092—dc21   00-066220   CIP   AC

Design by Stephanie Bart-Horvath
1 2 3 4 5 6 7 8 9 10
❖
FIRST EDITION

North Bridge

Concord

PAUL REVERE'S RIDE

Paul Revere was in a hurry. He ran down Boston's cobbled streets with hardly a sideward glance.

Silversmith, bell ringer, courier, and dentist, he was
rarely one to waste time. Now he had none to spare.

The British general Thomas Gage was also busy that evening—April 18, 1775. From his headquarters he issued many commands. One order was especially important: No one except his soldiers was to leave Boston that night.

Gage knew that the colonists had been gathering military supplies because they were upset at the way the British government ordered them around. The general had decided to seize some gunpowder and musket balls the colonists had stored in Concord, nineteen miles away. That would teach these so-called patriots a lesson.

But for this plan to succeed, no word must reach Concord ahead of the general's troops.

Someone, however, had already secretly sent a message to alert the colonists—including Paul Revere. Three riders had been chosen to spread the word all the way to Concord. He was one of them.

When Paul got home, he grabbed his boots while he told his wife, Rachel, the news. Rachel didn't want him to leave. It was too risky, she thought. Paul was a well-known messenger for the rebels. If he was caught, he might be thrown in jail or shot as a spy.

Paul knew that Rachel spoke the truth. But he was still determined to go.

Across town the British commander Lord Percy had received General Gage's orders. His boots and buckles gleamed as he reviewed the troops he was sending out. The seven hundred soldiers before him had been sitting around for months.

These British Regulars were eager to fight. But Lord Percy did not expect much trouble. The colonists grumbled about King George III's laws and taxes. But that didn't mean they would actually fight for their ideas against His Majesty's soldiers.

As Paul slipped through the streets, he dodged the roving British patrols. He had already ordered a friend to light two lanterns in a nearby church steeple. One lantern would have meant the British were taking the long way around by land. Two lanterns, however, meant they were leaving Boston by boat across the Charles River.

So even if Paul was captured, his fellow patriots would know which roads the British would take to Concord once they came ashore.

Paul planned to take a boat too. When he reached the river's edge, two men were waiting to row him across.

From Boston Common the British soldiers approached the Charles River in small groups, hoping to avoid any attention.

Twenty boats were waiting for them. There was no room to spare, and the soldiers huddled together like sticks. It took two crossings to ferry everyone to the other side.

When Paul and his rowers set out, the moon was
rising and long shadows stretched across the water.

They hugged the darkness, edging past a British war-
ship whose sentries were watching for trouble. The
three men barely dared to breathe as they passed near
the ship's many guns.

As the British Regulars left their boats, they trudged through marshy ground, spattering their scarlet coats and white breeches with mud. Back on dry land, they stood wet and uncomfortable, waiting for further orders.

A few soldiers sent out earlier were already guarding the roads. No spies, they thought, were going to slip past them that night.

Having reached the Charlestown shore, Paul was given a horse and set out at once. A few miles later two British soldiers on horseback jumped out from the shadows to confront him. One charged him directly. The other tried to block his retreat.

Paul did the only thing he could. He turned off the
road and galloped across the countryside. The soldiers
gave chase, but Paul had the fastest horse. He soon
left them behind.

Just before midnight Paul reached a house in Lexington where John Hancock and Samuel Adams were staying. He wanted to warn them of the soldiers' approach. If the redcoats found these two colonial leaders, they would surely take them prisoner.

Outside the house a sentry told him he was making too much noise. After all, the household was trying to sleep. "Noise!" Paul answered. "You'll have noise enough before long. The Regulars are coming out!"

And they were. As the British continued their march to Concord, two hundred men were sent on ahead to secure the road and bridges. Despite their attempts at secrecy, the soldiers could feel eyes watching them from the windows of the mostly darkened houses.

Just to be safe, the soldiers took prisoner any travelers they happened to meet.

Paul left Lexington with two other colonials on horseback. They had not gotten far before British soldiers stopped them. "If you go an inch further, you are a dead man," one said to Paul.

The other two riders managed to escape, but Paul was quickly surrounded. He was then questioned at gunpoint. He told the soldiers his name—which they recognized at once. He also declared that he knew their business, and that Concord had been warned of their coming.

This news made the soldiers anxious to rejoin their troops. They needed to move fast and didn't want to bother with a prisoner. So they took Paul's horse—and let him go.

When the British reached Lexington, a band of armed patriots was waiting for them. These Minutemen—as the colonists were called for their ability to gather quickly—did not want the soldiers to pass.

"Lay down your arms!" ordered the British commander.

Suddenly a shot was fired from somewhere. More shots followed. When the musket smoke cleared, eight colonials lay dead and another ten were wounded.

As the Minutemen tended to their fallen friends and neighbors, the British continued marching to Concord.

Paul Revere heard those shots because he had returned to Lexington on foot. He saw no fighting that day, but he did find out later what happened when the British troops reached Concord. Several hundred colonials were waiting by Concord's North Bridge. The two sides fought fiercely for hours. But the British finally gave up and began the long retreat back to Boston.

The next day Paul sneaked home to tell his family he was safe. But he didn't stay long, because the British were looking for him.

Soon the war actually started, and Paul carried many messages. He also printed money for the colonial rebels and commanded a fort in Boston Harbor.

When peace came at last, Paul went back to silversmithing. Later he sold hardware and ran a foundry. During the rest of his long and busy life, he approached everything the same way he had faced the night of his famous ride. He charged ahead—and never looked back.

When Paul Revere took his famous ride, the American colonists were angry because the British had imposed several taxes that the colonists thought were unfair. England, however, needed the money to support actions in other parts of its empire. The colonists were also upset that they were not allowed to elect their own representatives to Parliament. This left them victims of "taxation without representation."

More battles followed the fighting at Lexington and Concord. Fifteen months later, in July 1776, the colonies declared their independence from England, officially starting the American Revolution. Though the early victories were mostly British, the colonists never gave up. In 1781 the British suffered a major defeat at Yorktown, Virginia, and the war ended. A final peace was declared in 1783.

Over the years, Paul Revere's ride has come to be remembered, not only as a brave and valuable deed, but also as the symbolic moment when Americans first raised the alarm in defense of their freedom.